Dividing the Wayside

Dividing the Wayside

Jenny Haysom

Copyright © 2018 Jenny Haysom
All rights reserved

Palimpsest Press
1171 Eastlawn Ave.
Windsor, Ontario. N8S 3J1
www.palimpsestpress.ca

Book and cover design by Dawn Kresan. Printed in Ontario, Canada. Cover image by Sarah Hatton: *July 2* (Search Party). Oil, resin on panel, 2005. Photo credit: Pierre Laporte Photography.

Palimpsest Press would like to thank the Canada Council for the Arts and the Ontario Arts Council for their support of our publishing program. We also acknowledge the assistance of the Government of Ontario through the Ontario Book Publishing Tax Credit.

LIBRARY AND ARCHIVES CANADA CATALOGUING IN PUBLICATION

Haysom, Jenny, 1972–, author
    Dividing the wayside / Jenny Haysom.

Poems. Issued in print and electronic formats.
ISBN 978-1-926794-84-6 (SOFTCOVER)
ISBN 978-1-926794-85-3 (EPUB)
ISBN 978-1-926794-86-0 (KINDLE)
ISBN 978-1-926794-87-7 (PDF)

    I. TITLE.

PS8615.A858D58 2018   C811'.6   C2018-903225-1
                                                              C2018-903226-X

for Colin

Contents

11 Unfastened

I. Something Between Us

15 A Lesson
17 The Mite
18 First Death in Nova Scotia
19 A Chain Reaction
20 Our first apartment
21 Arrhythmia
22 Burning the Book (with my poems in it)
23 Memento
24 They say you can't go home again,
25 Spooked
26 Minnowing
27 Happy Birthday
28 Sized
29 Perspective
30 Keep to this Room
32 Reunion

II. Angel of Repose

35 Wherever I May Find Her:
36 House Tour
37 Artefacts
39 Herbarium
40 Dashes
42 Under Influence

43 Dear Master,
44 Last Respects
45 One Emily
46 Toward the Blue Peninsula

III. Stirring the Firmament

49 The New Colonialism
50 Reporting
51 Spin-off
52 Scrapyard
53 Lesser
54 Sticks
56 Stones
57 Waking in Larkin's *Aubade*
58 Invitation to Elizabeth Bishop
60 Unearthed
62 Haiku in March
63 Ostalgie
64 Four postcards and an umbrella from the Van Gogh Museum, Amsterdam
69 Wet Grass Blues
70 Haiku in June
71 The Minister of Loneliness
74 Saturday
75 Dürer's *Melencolia*
76 Ode to Consumption
77 His Nibs
78 Nightwalk
79 Vanitas

80	Beautiful Soup
82	The Winged Kama Sutra
83	Gargoyle
84	Henderson Island
85	Nocturne
86	Persona Albada

Notes
Acknowledgements
About the Author

Unfastened

A Roman fibula is not a bone
fluted with earth, but an ancient instrument
of closure. First born
 in Bronze Age fires, it alloyed
ornament with function—a sprung
 contrivance for brooching a cloak.

There is an eloquence in attachment
 I've heard before: tender buttons; a pop
of snaps; the quick pleasure in zippers
 realigning their tracks; and consider
Velcro biomimicking burrs....
 If only there were
such utility in poetry.

Something Between Us

A Lesson

My fourth-year Chaucer seminar
began with a lecture
on Love. The professor—
a small, bent man at the end of his tenure—
straightened and surveyed the wretched
lot of us, and declared
that there was no such thing
as Love, that what we suffered
was yearning, or lust. Long-suffering
he was, and intent on others
suffering too.

I knew his wife to be thrice
his size, a sumptuous woman
with a plunderable bosom. In her prime
she might have prowed a ship, or given a rousing
aria in the shower.

When I thought of lust, I pictured
my professor, young and yearning and thus
allured: an angular
insect on the nectar
of a plum.
        Poor him,
for he knew everything, yet somehow
he'd been tricked—and Love
was just a construct,
constructed
to affix.

That spring, we learned
how Romance was a sport—
no less—a courtly game like chess
in which a turreted Lady scorned
entreaty; of luting troubadours;
of Guillaume de Lorris
and Love's thorny, walled-in
allegory.
    And pent in our bodies, we read that rain
stirs the roots, that it is sweet
when Zephyr breathes, and Nature
pricks.

The Mite
—after Donne

Not stardust, just the ordinary stuff:
that screensaver gossamer of lint
and dander, each home's particular
detritus. Not what we are made of

but what we make in living, which is
a constant shedding we've undertaken
for more than twenty years together;
in sickness and squalor, co-wintering,

in growth or exuberance, our cells
bursting and twinkling then dwindling
like confetti. You might think it gross
that I picture us mingling, our skin

mixed in the gut of some blind,
microscopic arachnid, but this is love—
this dual diminishing—and I wish to mix
with you more, continuing, dust to dust.

First Death in Nova Scotia

Have you seen Nancy? My mother
took me by the shoulders
and shook me. Nancy

was younger, but in the country
it was common for children
of all ages to play together.

An unadulterated boredom
was our lot; gravel road
and level sea, the dour

fortitude of spruce. No doubt
there was a search party:
policemen silently

dividing the wayside, neighbours
flattening ferns in the wood.
All of us unravelling

the intricate perimeter, slick
of seaweed fringing rock,
where a child could

hop from outcrop to outcrop.

A Chain Reaction

When I was a girl I was kissed by a boy
    who suffered a near-fatal brain injury
a month later. When crossing the road
    from his house, he was hit by a car
and landed in the OR, then the ICU,
    his scalp sutured with staples that ran
like a zipper from crown to temple.
    In the hospital, he slept for a year
then awakened, and could barely say his name,
    or mine, when I finally saw him
at school. Pitied by teachers. Shunned
    by the kids who called him retarded.
I avoided him, sensed he sensed
    there was something between us
when he stared and stared from the thick
    windscreen of his forehead.
Afraid he might remember, I cruelly
    pretended I'd never much cared.

Our first apartment

was on Bland Street.
We painted the lathe and plaster
white, had barely any furniture.

Drafts and stains rose from the walls
like ghosts, and the place
was always a disaster.

No pets were allowed—except
for the mice. As the tenant below
was a drug dealer, visiting hours

were flexible. All night
the foghorn welled a note, like breath
blown in a bottle.

Arrhythmia

Remember the time we returned
to a flutter

behind the grate:
how we pried it open

and a starling flew in my face

then round the room, and out
the readied window

in a puff of Victorian soot
like the panicked

heart of Poe?

Burning the Book (with my poems in it)

Ragged, it torched the night like a meteor,
or a bat on fire, flapping. From the balcony

of our third apartment, we watched it fall
and fizzle in the juicy grass below. Beyond that,

a man and his dog stopped on the sidewalk. Anonymous,
they seemed to stand for something, so they stood

beneath the orange gloom of a streetlamp
and nonplussed, looked up at us.

Memento

In the early days, I knew you:
cupped in my belly, quiet
little snail. We went huddled

through the hard slap of winter,
and I imagined you, despite
white branches and the tundra sky.

When I made up my mind, the wind
snatched your one cry. I tried to ignore
the mute, featureless appeals, pretended

your magi were those lost explorers, wrapped
and frozen in their flags. Tonight, that cry
distinguishes itself from the mind's

regretful chorus. Your unborn
hair threads my ribs;
I wear you like a secret.

They say you can't go home again,

but we've had several homes, and two
gardens, and a weeping willow that wept
like a Roman fountain, and every so often

I do go back and survey the sites:
the door I painted yellow
painted white, reliable perennials

paved over, and the yard of dandelions
that matched the door,
gone also. Though most

we never owned, like the apartments
that lodged our younger selves—those indolent
shadow people

for whom I feel a parental
tenderness, now. And times
when I return, I stand and stare up

at soft shingles, at the square of dirty glass
from which we looked out: the homes
have prospered, no longer house

the likes of us—well, the sort
we used to be. So I reckon we've changed
but haven't changed, that selves

revise and yet maintain
their properties; that in our tenancies
we're alike, but estranged.

Spooked

There's old George, parked out front
on the no-parking side of the street, just
twelve feet from our front porch. His eyes reach

in through the window, while his wife
sits uncomfortably in the passenger seat.
Sometimes I picture him dismounting, popping

a warning shot aloft, then ordering me
off his property—the stuccoed, 30s semi
we bought six months ago. You see,

he left some things behind, a Canopic panoply
of himself: jars with rusty constituents, curious
coils of hose, and an array of wire coat hangers

all oddly reconfigured. This, and a whiff
in every cupboard, a doleful eau de cologne—hints
of nicotine and yesteryear, wakened like a fire.

Minnowing

Long-legged at the shore, she steps
and dips her net.
                  Across the lake, a heron
divines his dinner.

My daughter follows the minnows and their synchronous
shadows—sparks that dash and
turn like glitter, fountaining
out of reach.
            On the dock, a Mason jar
filled with lake-water, furnished with weeds, rocks and one fine
flake of mica—home for the day if your name is Topaz,
Flash or Pandora,
                  each fish—translucent—striped
deep in the centre with a miniature
backbone of silver.

I look up from my book,
                wish to capture
my daughter like this: intent
yet idle, her grace taken shape in time's
fluid material, there in the shallows—
minnowing—
                a weave of sunlight
loose at her ankles.

Happy Birthday

Lordy lordy, I lament—I'll never make the top forty
under forty. Should've pulled up my ducks
donkey's years ago—way back when
my oddness was fifty/fifty.
In that day and age,
hindsight missed
the boat at
20:20
.
Now
I take it
or heave it. Alas—
this isn't the bitter rind!
Confucius says that forty
is the new hermeneutic, and even if
I had been making poems hand over fist, no one
really knows if you can teach an old bird new lyrics.

Sized

I've had my grandmother's ring sized
to fit my finger, lessened
the work-etched

circumference to fit my smaller measure—
her hardships having
thickened her.

A baby daughter who died of fever.
A young son who succumbed
to pneumonia

while carried to the the doctor
on my grandfather's
shoulders.

My mother was third and a keeper:
born blue, but named
Barbara—

which means 'stranger.'

Perspective

Eyes on the trail: a worn
cradle of dirt and needles, ribbed
with roots and stomped
like a stable.
               Brash as flags our shirts
flash between
branches. In semaphore, single-
file, we ascend the tree line loud as sails and
winded to boot.

                       Lookout at the horizon:
blue sky/ blue
sea wavers like a hologram
levering the light.

Up here, the clouds
surround us, cumulus. We breathe in/
breathe out. Sublimate. Drift
off in puffs.

You say *here
today*, and *it's been years
in the making*. Together
we arrive at this perspective, lift
our heads, glimpse uncertain
origins, note
how far we've come—how high—
that beneath our feet these crowberries
plot the constellations.

Keep to this Room

Somehow, you'd persuaded the tooth fairy
to leave you loonies—and let you keep your milk teeth
too. One afternoon, while tidying your teenage room
I came upon them, almost forgotten: a small tin
of prospector's nuggets, and some fawn-coloured hair
from your first haircut, which I thought I'd thrown out.

I'm the one who throws things out.
You're the one who bargained with a fairy
and cried when I said she wasn't real. Your baby hair
is real, but now it's long and full. Your milk teeth
lost, yet cradled in a tin
and hidden in this room.

Growing up, you want a grownup room
even knowing that dolls must be thrown out
and the slipper-pink walls painted over. This tin
will remind you of what you've lost, for good, though a good fairy
once let you keep your teeth
and a plain snip of hair.

The Victorians liked a snip of hair.
They also kept shadowy rooms
and cleaned their teeth
with charcoal powder—or just pulled them out.
Like you, they believed in fairies
and would have locked them in tins

to prove that they were real. I have emptied my tins
or tried to empty them. I've swept hairs
from the baseboards, and wished for a house fairy
who would flit from room to room
like a feather duster, making regret disappear.
But what would she do with your teeth?

Victorian, could she fangle some heart-sick thing—all teeth
and woven hair? Perhaps she'd keep to this room,
guarded, and disappear when I opened the tin.

Reunion

Drunk as teenagers, we bared ourselves: out on the bluff
in a hot tub, rain off the Atlantic in strings flung
sideways, and some of us, as before,

getting it straight in the face. Gentlemen and children
were banished, and like desperate revellers
on a doomed cruise, we partied

into the storm. The next night we returned, verging
on sober, a tempest spent, the ceiling
starfall. In the dark our bodies

harboured what had been, and though we'd changed,
what remained was hardly fate, but something
sadly resolved.

Angel of Repose

> We do not play on Graves—
> Because there isn't Room—
> Besides—it isn't even—it slants
> And People come—
>
> —EMILY DICKINSON (467)

Wherever I May Find Her:

Shuttered in the yellow homestead
riding on her scrolled sleigh bed.

In the parlour pressing petals.
Tearing pages from the hymnals.

Speaking from behind the door
to inquiring visitors—or

circumventing household chores
and sliding down the banister.

Off singing with the Bobolink.
Crying over spilled ink

in a dress of paper white.
In a certain slant of light.

Like a genie—transcendental—
bottled in a humble pebble

or a drop of dew—held captive—
and after rain—a mist—refracted.

On a summer afternoon,
in the rafters—falling through—

or lying underneath the grass
listening to our footsteps pass.

House Tour

Pilgrim, I stand in your parlour:
to imagine you here one must ignore
the props, and listen. Outside, heaven
weighs like a cloche. A fly on the sill
awakens.

Next, we ascend to your chamber
where a table and chair
invite in the corner. And who wouldn't wish
to lie down on your sleigh bed—
harness their dreams to your mares?

Artefacts

*

Because it followed her around
And echoed every step—
Or guided—as a Compass could—
Her Solitary Ship.

Compelling like a metronome,
As if a life—might slip—
She did not quell it in the dark
For fear that it would stop.

*

To Clarify her Enterprise
She wore a dress of white:
Material—as milk and eggs—
And Mystical as Light.

Mornings she did put it on—
And evenings—she removed.
A page to place her thoughts upon—
To Pose—or else—Delete—

*

A hanky of a desk—
But eighteen inches square.
Beneath the Plank of cherrywood
An Elementary drawer.

Inside the single drawer—
Her fascicles of Verse,
And in each little Scripture,
A Speaker—issued—since—

*

As if her portrait were a pool
Reflecting other girls—
a liquor so Mercurial
That we can see—Ourselves.

Herbarium

Wake-Robin—Heliotrope—Venus's Looking-glass.
Bedstraw—Yellow Flag and Blue-eyed Grass.

Hispid Buttercup plus Interrupted Fern.
Birdfoot Violet. Wintergreen.

Virgin's Bower. Arrowhead or Witherod.
Jack-in-the-Pulpit—Bastard Toadflax—Spotted

Touch-Me-Not.

Poison Ivy—Toothwort and Privet.
Barberry and Dogbane and Catnip.

Lily-of-the-Valley—Queen-of-the-Meadow.
Scarlet Indian Paintbrush—Wild Indigo.

Smoketree—Candle Larkspur—Climbing
Fumitory. Nightshade. Starflower. Winged

Everlasting—

Dashes

vectors veering—there
to here—
        bridges hinging
spheres—
        they're logs for crossing
boggy spots or high wires
between stars—

omissions—chinks—
gaps and clefts—
pauses—breaks—
or blinks
and breaths—

they're insect bits
on window ledges—needles
dripped from
hemlock hedges—

filings—whiskers—
figments—splinters—

naughts—and crosses
halved—
        they're atoms
flattened—arms outstretched—

harpoons and spears
and gaffs—

strata stitched—mental shrapnel—
heartbeats—hiccups—

—matter straddled—

choreography—for bees—

component parts
or locks and keys—scattered
tines from dandelions—

axles—spokes
and spindles—

leaps or skips—and snips
of twine—

ladders
disassembled—

they're intersections—changed
directions—pangs
and inclinations—
                        a willful
blemish—fallen
eyelash—
        air's
articulation—

Under Influence

At first subtle, she arose,
icy and tidal, entering my shoes
at the toe. Thus introduced

she deluged
the rest, wet each thread
through capillarity. Willingly,

I went further, spiralled
down steps to the cool
vault of her thoughts:

once in that cellar
I tippled—inspired—and
swallowed the dark.

Dear Master,

I wait—and still no answer—
The Hours blank as snow.
No word of you—no letter—
No telegraph come through.

You think that I'd know better
For there is Naught—to know—
Enclosed in Alabaster
lest my Gist gets through.

A substance dry as Winter—
I mystify the dew—
In essence—High—as Ether—
Our final rendezvous.

Last Respects

A downpour paused, and now we squash around
these weedy humps. Our black umbrellas
folded down, the air gone pale as milk.

Our maps say here, but here's
an acre—more—a vacant square
of mounds and slabs and sepulchres

and which one hers?
Like crows, we poke and peer,
recite the names as some inverted roll call

spanning years. At last, you cry across the yard—
and there: *her* name through iron tines, a bedstead
for our angel of repose.

We stop. Then step from foot
to foot. Beneath, the turf has thinned to mud
where those like us have trod—and stood.

One Emily

Dour in daguerrotype, and fit
for a funeral. A taut
frill at her throat. Backbone
straight as a steeple.
No simple chorus girl, our belle
of Amherst. Now the impostors
bustle in: those ink-eyed
lookalikes and shrinking
violets, a waltz of wallflowers
humming hymns. How unfaithful
our flirtations—wanting more
than we've been given—when
to Dwell in Possibility is the closest
clime to heaven.

Toward the Blue Peninsula
   —after a box made by Joseph Cornell

Gridded, rationed, it is a cupboard
swept of crumbs. Window open,
perch ready for the bird to come.
All we can do is anticipate—

though perhaps it's been
and gone. What we have instead
is space visited; a passing-through
to blue distances—archived.

Like a thought in an empty room.
Or a room—emptied—
so we can think. Come in
from cluttered hours, curl toes
around the rail, test our heads in apertures
or look out the window and stare:

Stirring the Firmament

The New Colonialism

Legend has it that Jimi Hendrix released
a mating pair, an Adam and Eve, from the balcony
of his Carnaby Street apartment in the 60s.
Others claim they flew the coop in '51, jettisoned

from Isleworth Studios upon completion
of the English scenes of equatorial peril
in *The African Queen*. Regardless of what one
believes, there are presently more than thirty

thousand ring-necked parakeets in London
and environs. On Primrose Hill, in Kensington
Gardens, neon-green denizens are infiltrating
trees. They're picking new grass in suburban

pockets; infringing, like weeds between paving;
and punctuating the quiet good taste of grey
with their raucous squeaks and loud livery. Parakeets
are a splurge on polite society, upsetting

delicate breeds at the feeder and threatening
native species. Consequently, the British Government
has decreed the feral parrot a pest, and placing it
on a shortlist, agrees that the birds can be shot.

Reporting

The footage in the news seems a further
indignity: two girls strung from a mango tree,
robed in fuchsia and green, turning
in the heat, as the villagers

gather at their dusted feet. In their forms
I see a ripening. Young shoulders
yoked by collarbones, each limb
a length of silk. Untouchables—

but fourteen and fifteen—gang-raped
in the fields, their bodies hoisted
as quarry. Now the sun stares equitably
while the villagers grieve. Khakied policemen threaten

and shrug. One of the fathers cries angrily
for the cameras, but the mothers
crouch in the dirt, in the shadowed huts
with their faces covered.

Spin-off

Discovery of plastic-eating caterpillar could prove a boon in waste disposal, reads the headline. The photo:
a crinkly polybag nibbled

to tatters, and our sin-eaters—creamy, well-upholstered
waxworms—chewing their pseudo
cabbage leaf

like any other grub. But what of birds who pluck them?
Will plasticky larvae lodge
in their guts,

indissoluble, like slugs of chewing gum? Or the moths
blossoming in lurid colours, compelled
to melt against porch lights?

Scrapyard

A blue afternoon
and the gulls
patrol. No fish heads
or dumpster grub
here, yet they angle
and circle, stirring
the firmament,
ready as angels
to salvage. Beneath,
forklifts and cranes
travail, and a giant claw
stacks wrecks
in polychrome
layers. Like mattresses
in a futurist
fairytale, piled high
for the shallow
sleep of automatons,
a strata in which one
white feather
—shrewdly inserted—
might awaken something
or someone.

Lesser

They'd supposed it the size of an economy car—
but when a great blue whale washed ashore
in Newfoundland, its heart was smaller.
More like a piano. Merely a golf cart.
They were in search of a fitting metaphor.
Pathologists wading through gore to the waist,
a fetor of decay that was less of a smell—more of a taste.

Sticks

My first
was a squirrel-torn
twig of Magnolia, its buds
furred and full
and sensual.
        The next had a tight-lipped
obscurity; a wind-ripped
bough from a city tree, set upon
my path, obliquely.

And there were many—each branch
brought home and planted in water, like an antler
or a limb from a creature
that could calmly
grow another.

It can take hours
or days or
weeks.
        Some tips swelling quickly
in furnace-fed, time-lapse
photography,
            while others
rouse drowsily—a slow and invisible
fulfillment.

Then rupture, the first
unfurlings: tiny green pennants
trumpet their victory; yellowish arrowheads
stipple and spar; some sawtoothed hearts
graze the air.

You might say that my house is a sanctuary
for sticks, each one an orphan,
a pyrotechnician.
                      When yesterday
I turned my back—a sudden
chartreuse detonation.

Stones

Late March, 1941. Virginia Woolf
put her overcoat on, filled the pockets
with stones and stepped into the river
in the hope that it would hold her.

On occasion, I have handled
those stones: placid as paperweights/
mindful as moons. Each a decision
measured in the palm.

Waking in Larkin's *Aubade*

I can't believe it
when I open my eyes—and
what happened last night?

All around me, the singular
props of a 50s bachelor:
modest pornography, the jumpy

telephone, and an emptied
wardrobe that yawns and reveals
a static tinkle of hangers. No note,

but he left me a poem
about getting drunk
and blanking out. Next to me,

his pillow indented—and there
a pair of eyeglasses that
ogle back, vacantly.

Invitation to Elizabeth Bishop

From Great Village by Greyhound
traversing all things provincial,
    please come riding.
Through the fog of a thousand boiling kettles
or a reserve of tears unfettered as drizzle,
    please come riding.
Lulled by the tidal murmur of readers
rising from lamp-lit harbours
on a night both strange and familiar,
    please come riding.

A crazy quilt of stars will chart
your expedition, and the breakers will glisten
with phosphorescent jots
of punctuation. With your suitcase
packed with syllables, and your pockets full
of loaves and fishes/ crumbs and miracles,
    please come riding.

If not by bus, arrive
astride the majesty
of a moose. From roadside
stands of spruce, emerge
like a Maritime mahout, twigs
snagged in the wool of your hair
and mayflowers trailing. Scribbled
with cobwebs, advancing
in zigzags, please—
    please come riding.

And if you cannot come riding
      come in writing,
a noonday ghost, a shadow on the page
inclining. Or with pails of blueberries
at your sides—though not for baking—
but for an afterlife's supply
of the mystical, purplish
      ink you're formulating.

Unearthed

I found it on the dirt—the shucked
capsule of some kind of beetle, its back
hunched and segmented and primal
as a fossil. I lifted it on my trowel

and held it to the light: translucent,
but tinted brown, like crackling Sellotape
unsticking from the spine of a yellowed
novel, and clinging to this, fine

crumbs of soil. Earthling,
I thought, examining the carapace
in all its facets, the forelegs hooked
and barbed as a scarab's. Something

grounded, trundling ground
or tunnelling it, and the wrapper
a memento of this. Days later, a second
discovery: a luminous cicada

low on the trunk of a tree, and beneath it
another husk, riven and affixed
to the bark. So this was it—Basho's
shell which had sung itself

utterly away, but hadn't yet sung,
if you call that tinnitus song. Long
had I puzzled this, the poet's mascot
a rackety thing, in hundreds

buzzing like ethereal power tools
from August's luscious treetops.
The whine to which I scuffed
the dust. A deafening backdrop

to blinding afternoons. I'd once found one
on the sidewalk, discharged
from the sooty canopy, dark and dry
and ailing, like an electron

out of orbit, it hardly resembled
this newest thing, this green
compression—its folded wings
tightly creased as origami.

Haiku in March

Birds on the wires bead
an abacus, and I count
the days before spring.

Ostalgie

Across the street from the Checkpoint Charlie replica
you can buy Eastern memorabilia: ushankas
of dubious fur, flags with the hammer and sickle,
Trabi dinky cars or Stasi pins and buckles...
just about anything DDR—

and most of it made in China. In the souvenir shops
a rainbow array of concrete nuggets; bits chipped
by the *mauerspechte*—wallpeckers—whose chisels
beneficently worked the divide, looting
history for what it's worth.

Four postcards and an umbrella from the Van Gogh Museum, Amsterdam

i. Sunflowers

Simple, yet intricately pupilled, these flowers
are for you. Each vase of orbital blooms
heavy with earthen hues:

impasto of ochre, chrome
and cadmium, Naples and Indian
yellow; our joyous poisons of the palette.

Though palatable, honeyed—colour of maize
and mustard seed. Each stroke a smudge
of butter, a greasy

yellow fever. Dear friend,
fellow painter: may you awaken
to such open faces, feel yourself the sun of their attention

as they follow you across the room.

ii. Self-Portrait with Bandaged Ear

I didn't see
what happened, but I was listening
comme toujours. And it's true, there was a row; words
whopped the air like boxer's blows.

Someone gonged the frying pan, another
clapped the door. Papers startled—
curled into corners. The empty cupboard
groaned. They were up too close in that yellow house

yet Vincent was alone. Who knows
who was coerced, or if his own disquiet
buzzed like flies around a horse.
Some say I made him do it—and of course

I was there. We ears always are;
pink, protuberant, aware.
Even while you rest
we keep watch, as it were.

iii. Almond Blossom

Some of us carry a cloud, but this awning is far more precipitous;
so much depends upon branches—these petals
upheld in quintuplicate.

iv. Sower with Setting Sun

Faceless, this labourer, whose crude hand
drizzles grains of indigo and ochre. Farmer

or saviour, his corona a sun
yoked to the day's endeavours.

And who is this painter
plying the last light? Blue field/

green sky. The clouds distantly
pink. A man is to sow if he is later to pick.

v. Wheatfield with Crows

I stand alone before a field of wheat. At my back, the wind blows
steadily, ushering clouds, their shadows lapsing past
in spooked herds. My brush daubs the horizon
but cannot reach, bristles with phthalo,
cobalt, and holy ultramarine.
                                    In this air
thinned with turpentine, a cry—
was that me?
                Unsettled, the crows
fly off, and the wheat
bows and heaves
as all things
depart.

Wet Grass Blues

My neighbour mows his lawn in the rain, curses
in Hebrew, having never grown up with grass.

Mild man, I picture the child in a dusty yard, his homeland
shifting like sand and stars.
                                        No minefield here but turf
turned meadow, his ploughshare gassed, a monster chew of
stick and bone, as there are dog-toys strewn
in this Kentucky blue, all green
with rain.

Haiku in June

It rained for days, the hours
curtained. Windows
framed our introspections.

The Minister of Loneliness

has no ministry—just an office
and a phone. She sleeps diagonally
on cool sheets, her blinds raised
to the moon. Mornings,

the Minister forsakes alarms
and wakes to the low coo of pigeons
shuffling in the sun. She takes
breakfast on the go: espresso

and a raisin bun (how she hates
raisins, picks them out, one
by one, drops them on the pavement
where people step on them).

The walk to work is her favourite
time of day, when solitariness
seems the perfect state: swept air,
emptied streets—just the way

the janitor left them—and the odd
person going about his business
independently. She strides
purposefully over bridges, past

the padlocked sweethearts without
a pause or pang, swinging
her empty portfolio, planning
a February getaway to some

distant archipelago. It's only
when she arrives that her prospects
dim. That grim little office.
The thought of yet another day

with a hole puncher. *Don't despair*
says a yellow Post-it note
affixed to the window
facing the parking lot. Once

an attendant practised his cello there
in a narrow booth. Now you slot
your chit in an automated
wicket—and the arm lifts by itself.

At least the Queen of Loneliness
has a kingdom. Someone joked
and called her swivel chair
The Throne of Isolation. For hours

on end she swivels there, painting
her nails blue or black, or that
minty shade: *tristesse.*
Loneliness

only crosses her mind or desk
by way of dockets and memos,
as long anonymous letters
from her multitudinous constituents

that can't be answered.
After all, she has no staff,
no ministry. If misery loves
company, she has no love.

Saturday

All morning flurries fell like ashes
and time accrued, the piling slow.
Our installations—breakfast dishes.
Papers stacked the news askew.

As time accrued, the piling slow,
we sat and read—and checked our watches.
Papers stacked the news askew
and furred our fingertips with ashes.

We sat and read and checked our watches
as time was emulating snow.
Our fingertips were faintly tarnished.
Our spirits tinged with déjà-vu.

While time was emulating snow
our languishing became pernicious:
the library books were overdue
and dust accrued on every surface.

We didn't have a thing to show
but counters heaped with breakfast dishes,
a listlessness, some fallen snow,
our litter piling up like wishes.

Dürer's *Melencolia*

Through the hourglass
the hours pour. She sits and
twiddles her caliper.

Ode to Consumption

Those dust-ruffled poets suffered it, a land-locked
drowning, or just the threat of inclement
death that could swallow you
slowly.
      In those days, she was a conventional beauty—
an anaemic girl who lingered at riversides, waiting, her tresses
camouflaged in the willow's
candelabrum.
              Not everyone who passed
saw her. You had to have the right
disposition; an ear for unheard song, a tongue
for deep-casked draughts, and an eye for loitering
dryads.
      She was there
if you looked—and who could blame a boy
for looking?
              Perhaps in a moment's indolence
he stopped too long, leaned
too far, and saw not a girl
but himself:
           closed lids
cast in plaster, his own lips
sans merci.

His Nibs

In 1746, the Swedish king gave Carolus Linnaeus
a pet raccoon, a sentient trinket of New World
wilderness. Unsurprisingly, our Father of Taxonomy
was enamoured of his companion, named him
Sjupp, then spoiled the rapscallion with all manner
of treats and indulged his thieving proclivities.

By all accounts, Sjupp had an obstinate character.
Like a toddler, he abhorred a tether, and would strain
or just sit when led. Still, Linnaeus grieved
when the unfettered creature was killed by a dog,
but soon got over it, and with slab and scalpel
dissected him (to better categorize his nibs).

Nightwalk

Procyon, bright star of the constellation
Canis minor—an underdog,
lesser dog, that heels

to the hunter Orion. By skyglow, as city lights
shun heaven's, the lesser *Procyon lotor*
perambulates

on the leather flats of his delicate feet
and leaves greasy tracks
on the tarmac.

Vanitas

*

Fine brushstrokes are required
to impart the black sheen of this perished
squirrel, opened like an evening bag, its glittering
contents spilled.
      A crow arrives, scatters
a wriggling, blue-green pavé of flies to reveal
the actual insides: a shock
of pink.

*

From a distance, it might be a shred of blown-out tire
cornered in the gutter, and up close,
a scrap of boot leather.

You wouldn't recognize the squirrel
but for the fluff that was once a tail.

*

We can't entirely avoid it, but I buffer you
from the sight of a dead squirrel
who's eyeing us.
      If van Eyck
were to paint this, he'd make that eye
a mirror, a looking glass
      whose convex exterior
captures the subject of the picture,
which is me, and you—a child
who already recognizes
that look.

Beautiful Soup

Sand Pits Lake was once a quarry, the ground scooped
deep as a tureen. If you flipped it, would it say
bone china, or *dishwasher safe*?
I float on my back,

the water green and mottled as turtle soup. A lady breaststrokes by
in sunglasses and straw hat, her chin held high,
while grazing the surface, some spidery
seedfluff, dragonflies.

It has a certain magic—a music. You can almost hear
a string quartet accompany the matron,
and if you squint your eyes
we might all be

bathers of the archetypal kind; anonymous, impressionist, near-
naked figures in an Edenic scene, one Sunday
afternoon, the trees bent over
like long-necked animals

come to drink. Yet glimpsed within, fugitive licks of orange
in brash counterpoise—koi fattened
to an unnatural size on local
fauna, each fish

thick as your thigh. Too big for the tank, the garden pond,
then dumped in the lake to swim with us. Round
and round, they scour the basin as if
this were another enclosure

they've outgrown. And how will they overwinter?
Face to the sun, I picture them: deep
in torpor, fanning dark water, live
as embers beneath the ice.

The Winged Kama Sutra

Damselflies:
some girls/ some
guys. Above the lake they skim—hover—light on
water. Filaments. All
fire & eyes.

One
stops to rest—wings
pressed in prayer. Two lock together. Black
lace and
wire.

So many
positions—no missionary
fare: Arched Reflection; Tiptoe on Head; Needle Threads
Needle; Stick-up Mid-
air.

Gargoyle

From Old French, meaning
gullet or throat. When heaven
opens, damnation spouts.

Henderson Island

One of the world's most remote places... is also one of its most polluted.
—THE GUARDIAN

On this coral atoll in the South Pacific, the castaways
are synthetic. Palms shush above
the wreckage

where hundreds of hermit crabs
find refuge. Some carry
bottle caps

instead of seashells. Others retire to cosmetic pots
of blanched polyethylene, and one
is reported

to have taken up in a doll's head
that gazes at the sun
and criss-

crosses the sand,
sidestepping
trash.

Nocturne

This is what they call The Dark, so dark
that you can touch it—reach out and poke
the planets, feel the air

slide through your fingers like fine strands of hair.
And the lake below is darker yet, a deeper
black: the colour of absence that's always there.

Down here, down here. You hear it
in your sleep, its lapping appetite, the black lake
with a nocturnal call, throwing its voice

at the door, again and again. You open
that door and step out. Or is it in?
In the dark, hands out—

however useless they are—two pale
diurnal creatures at night, vulnerable
as star-nosed moles above the soil, or salamanders

spotted by flashlight.

Persona Albada

Dream's disciple, I rise, go down to the lake in answer:
no one here, but a stretch of water as taut
as a sheet awaiting a sleeper.

A turtle punctures the sky, his head a polished stone.
Haloed, he glistens for an instant in the sun
until I move and he's gone.

Notes

"Herbarium" is something of a found poem. When she was a teenager, Emily Dickinson pressed plants and flowers and mounted them in an extensive herbarium with scientific names. I have taken a very small selection of her specimens and given them back their common names, then organized these names into a kind of narrative.

"Dear Master," is the only poem in the sequence that assumes ED's point of view. Shortly after her death, three draft letters addressed to "Master" were discovered among her papers. Though there are many theories, no one has been able to identify who this addressee was (a lover? God?).

"One Emily" was inspired by a news story. Shortly after my pilgrimage to the Dickinson homestead in Amherst, Massachusetts (August 2012), ED was in the headlines. Following months of analysis, a daguerreotype was released to the public, one that was—according to some experts—a second photographic image of the poet. Throughout the years, a number of contenders have been considered and dismissed, but this likeness is the most convincing yet.

"Toward the Blue Peninsula" is an ekphrastic piece about one of Joseph Cornell's boxes by the same title, which in turn refers to a Dickinson poem (405). Cornell made several boxes in homage of ED.

"Reporting" makes reference to a 2014 incident in Katra, in the northern Indian state of Uttar Pradesh. Two Dalit girls—cousins, ages fourteen and fifteen—were gang-raped and murdered, their bodies strung from a tree in the centre of the village by their assailants.

"Spin-off" quotes a 2017 headline from the CBC news website.

"Lesser" describes the autopsy of a Great Blue Whale that came ashore in Newfoundland in 2014. ROM scientists gave fascinating accounts of the project and struggled to find a metaphor to convey the actual size of the whale's heart. I have included some of their similes in the poem.

"Ostalgie" is a portmanteau, a German term that combines the words "nostalgie" (nostalgia) and "ost" (east). It is a peculiar nostalgia for life in East Germany under Soviet rule, and also a word for the popular memorabilia and souvenirs that reflect this.

"Sunflowers" is a study in yellow—the most poisonous colour of the painter's palette—and Vincent van Gogh's favourite. In anticipation of his guest, Paul Gauguin, he painted multiple canvases of sunflowers to decorate the Yellow House in Arles. Two of these adorned the walls of Gauguin's bedroom, including the most astonishing of the compositions, which featured yellow flowers in a yellow vase against a yellow background. To his brother, Theo, van Gogh wrote: "I'm painting with the gusto of a Marseillais eating bouillabaisse, which won't surprise you when it's a question of painting large sunflowers."

"Almond Blossom" is an imagist ode to our new umbrella. Van Gogh completed this Japanese-inspired painting during his voluntary stay at an asylum in Saint Rémy. It was a gift for his baby nephew, named Vincent. As well as celebrating the beauty of new life, it also depicts its fragility.

"The Minister of Loneliness" actually doesn't have a ministry—the rest is playful speculation (on a serious subject and a growing societal problem). The position was created by the British Government in memory of murdered Labour MP, Jo Cox, and an appointment was made in January 2018.

"Nightwalk" features the star *Procyon*, whose name comes from the Greek and means "before the dog." Interestingly, the scientific name for the common raccoon is *Procyon lotor*. Like humans—but unlike dogs—raccoons walk on the soles of their feet.

"Beautiful Soup" comes from the Mock Turtle's song in Lewis Carroll's *Alice's Adventures in Wonderland*.

"Henderson Island" was inspired by a news story. According to *The Guardian* (May 2017), this uninhabited island "has been found by marine scientists to have the highest density of anthropogenic debris recorded anywhere in the world, with 99.8% of the pollution plastic."

"Persona Albada" plays on the Latin term *persona non grata*, an unwelcome person, and the Spanish word "albada," which is a song or composition performed at the break of day—and also a root word for "aubade."

Acknowledgements

A number of poems in this book have previously appeared in the following journals: *Arc Poetry Magazine*, *Dusie*, *CV2*, *The Fiddlehead*, *The New Quarterly* and *The Walrus*. I would like to extend my thanks to the dedicated teams—paid and voluntary—working for these publications.

The poem "Minnowing" inspired an original piece of music written by Scott Richardson. This composition was performed by Scott (on piano), and by soprano Doreen Taylor-Claxton in 2012, for one of the Ottawa New Music Creators concerts.

Additionally, a selection from this manuscript was published in chapbook form (*Blinding Afternoons*: Anstruther Press, 2017). A big thank you to editor Jim Johnstone for his kindness and ongoing support.

For the editing and design of this book—inside and out—I'd like to thank Dawn Kresan. The cover art is an early painting by visual artist Sarah Hatton from a series entitled "Search Party."

Many thanks… to Steven Heighton for showing me the ropes, years ago, and for reading and commenting on most of the poems in this collection. To Brian Bartlett, my first creative writing teacher. In memory of Terry Whalen, whose passion for poetry made a lasting impression. To my former and current writing groups, The Other Tongues and Ruby Tuesdays, for their critiques and camaraderie. To David O'Meara, for helping organize an unruly manuscript; Don McKay, for reading and listening at Piper's Frith; and Alison Goodwin, for being a true poet-friend.

Deepest gratitude and love to my daughter, Lucy, and husband, Colin.

The following poems have dedications: "Minnowing" and "Keep to this Room" are for Lucy. "The Mite" and "Perspective" are for Colin. "Sized" is for Annie and Barbara, and "Reunion" is for Alison.

I would also like to acknowledge the support of an Ontario Arts Council Recommender Grant.

About the Author

Jenny Haysom was born in England and raised in Nova Scotia. She completed her Master's degree in English Literature at the University of Ottawa and has since worked for independent booksellers and the Ottawa Public Library. Her writing has been widely published and she is *Arc Poetry Magazine*'s former prose editor.